WELCOME TO MY World

CLOTHES

Around the World

by Ellen Lawrence

Ruby Tuesday Books

Published in 2026 by Ruby Tuesday Books Ltd.

Editor: Mark J. Sachner
Design & Production: Tammy West

Photo credits:
Alamy: Cover (Yadid Levy), 13 (Jake Lyell), 16 (Roberto Cornacchia), 17 (Hemis); Arctic Photos: 10–11; Cephoto, Uwe Aranas: 7TR, 22; FLPA: 5 (left); Public Domain: 7BR, 22; Shutterstock: 4L (Tatyana Vyc), 4C (altanaka), 4R (Celso Pupo), 5TR (idome), 5BR (Maksim Dubinsky), 6L (Hurst Photo), 6R (meunierd), 7TL (Monkey Business Images), 8 (Mark Green), 9 (Cinematographer), 12L (GreenTree), 12R (Don Mammoser), 14L (Ninafotoart), 14C (Flashon Studio), 14R (Damian Hadjiyvanov), 15L (wdeon), 15TR (Kobby Dagan), 15BR (Vicki L. Miller), 18 (Franco Lucato), 19L & 19BR (Kanokratnok), 19TR (Sandra van der Steen), 20L (Daniel Prudek), 20C (Steffen Foerster), 20R, 21TL, 21BL (ESB Professional), 21R (Anton Ivanov); Uniesert: 7BL, 22.

Library of Congress Control Number: 2024949049
Hardback ISBN 978-1-78856-537-0
Paperback ISBN 978-1-78856-538-7
ePub ISBN 978-1-78856-539-4

Published in Minneapolis, MN
Printed in the United States

www.rubytuesdaybooks.com

The picture on the front cover of this book shows children from Peru. Turn to page 8 to find out more about the colorful clothes they are wearing.

CONTENTS

Clothes Are Important 4
Clothes for School 6
Rainbow Quechua Clothes 8
Warm Reindeer Clothes 10
Colorful Indian Saris 12
Traditional Clothes 14
A Special Headdress 16
Colorful Maasai Shukas 18
We All Love T-Shirts! 20
Welcome to My World 22
Glossary 23
Index 24

Words shown in bold in the text are explained in the glossary.

All the places in this book are shown on the map on page 22.

Clothes Are Important

We all wear clothes every day. But how do we choose which clothes to wear?

On cold days, we choose clothes that keep us warm.

On hot days, we choose clothes that keep us cool.

We choose clothes that show we love our team!

We choose clothes that show who we are.

We wear clothes that show what we believe.

Clothes for School

Every morning, children around the world get dressed for school. Many children wear a school uniform.

These children in the United States wear their regular clothes for school.

These children in Nairobi, in Kenya, wear red sweaters for school.

Most kids in the United Kingdom wear a school uniform.

Girls going to school in Malaysia

These school uniforms in Brazil show off the colors of the country's flag.

These kids are on their way to school in India.

Rainbow Quechua Clothes

High in the Andes Mountains in Peru, Quechua people raise sheep, alpacas, and llamas.

They dye the wool from their animals.

Then they use it to **weave** and knit colorful fabrics and clothes.

Quechua women and girls wear skirts and jackets made from wool.

Weaving with wool

Men and boys wear ponchos and hats with earflaps called *chullos*. It's **traditional** for a father to knit a baby's first chullo.

Warm Reindeer Clothes

In freezing, icy Siberia, Nenets people wear warm clothes made from reindeer skins and fur.

The Nenets are reindeer **herders**.

They move from place to place finding food for their animals.

Nenets women sew reindeer skins together to make warm clothes and boots.

Reindeer skin boots

A reindeer skin coat is made from the skins of several different reindeer. It may have fur on the inside or on the outside.

Colorful Indian Saris

In India, women and girls wear saris.

A sari is a long piece of brightly colored cloth.

A sari is draped around the body and over the head to give many different looks.

Saris have been worn in India for more than 2,000 years.

These girls are wearing highly decorative saris at a festival.

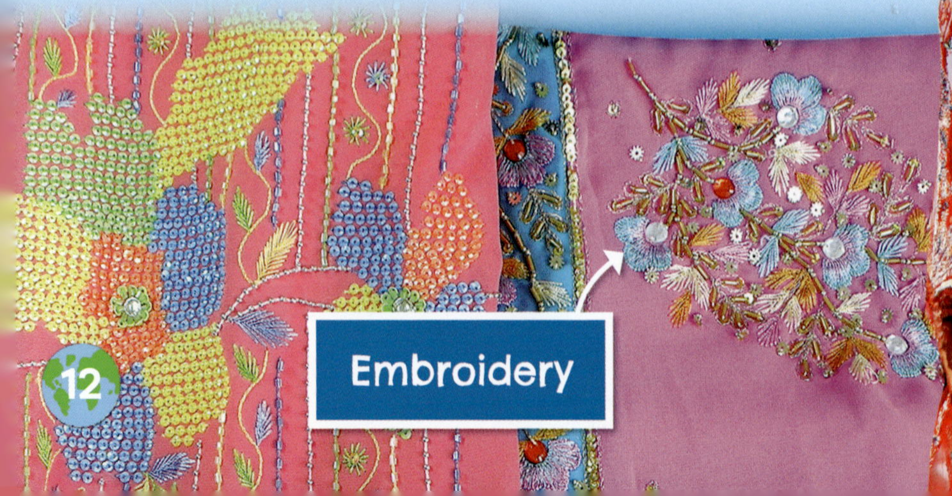

Embroidery

Under a sari, women and girls wear a long skirt.

They also wear a short, tight-fitting blouse called a *choli*.

Some saris are plain, while others are decorated with **embroidery**, beads, and even tiny mirrors. A sari can be up to 27 feet (8 m) long.

Traditional Clothes

Sometimes we wear traditional or special clothes to celebrate a festival or holiday.

A traditional costume from Bulgaria

Some traditional clothing looks like the clothes our **ancestors** wore.

These girls are at a festival on the island of Tenerife, Spain.

During the Kwanzaa festival, African Americans proudly wear clothes from their ancestors' homelands in Africa.

Every year, hundreds of Native American **powwows** are held across North America. At a powwow, Native people celebrate the traditions of their ancestors. They also celebrate the culture of their tribes today.

A Special Headdress

The Long Horn Miao people live in China.

For special occasions and festivals, women and girls wear dramatic headdresses.

To create her headdress, a girl attaches a pair of wooden horns to her head.

Next, a large bundle of fabric, black wool, and real hair is placed on the horns.

Wooden horns

The bundle is tied with a long, white ribbon.

Long Horn Miao women have very long hair. That's because once a girl is 18, she never cuts her hair again. The real hair in a girl's headdress is from her female ancestors.

Colorful Maasai Shukas

The grasslands of Tanzania and Kenya are home to the Maasai people.

They wear clothes in bright colors—especially red!

A shuka

Maasai people wear a cloak around their shoulders called a *shuka*.

A shuka may be just one color, or it can have a striped or checked pattern.

The color red is a sacred color to the Maasai people. This means it is very important to their beliefs. They believe that red helps keep them safe from wild animals, such as lions.

Maasai people make and wear lots of jewelry made of beads.

Maasai boys wearing shukas

Sandals made from car tires

We All Love T-Shirts!

What colorful, comfortable piece of clothing do kids wear all around the world?

It's the T-shirt!

If you outgrow your favorite T-shirt, you can give it to a **charity**. The charity may send it to another country where people need clothes. Your T-shirt will become another kid's favorite piece of clothing!

Nepal

Ecuador

Australia

Vietnam

Canada

Ghana

Welcome to My World

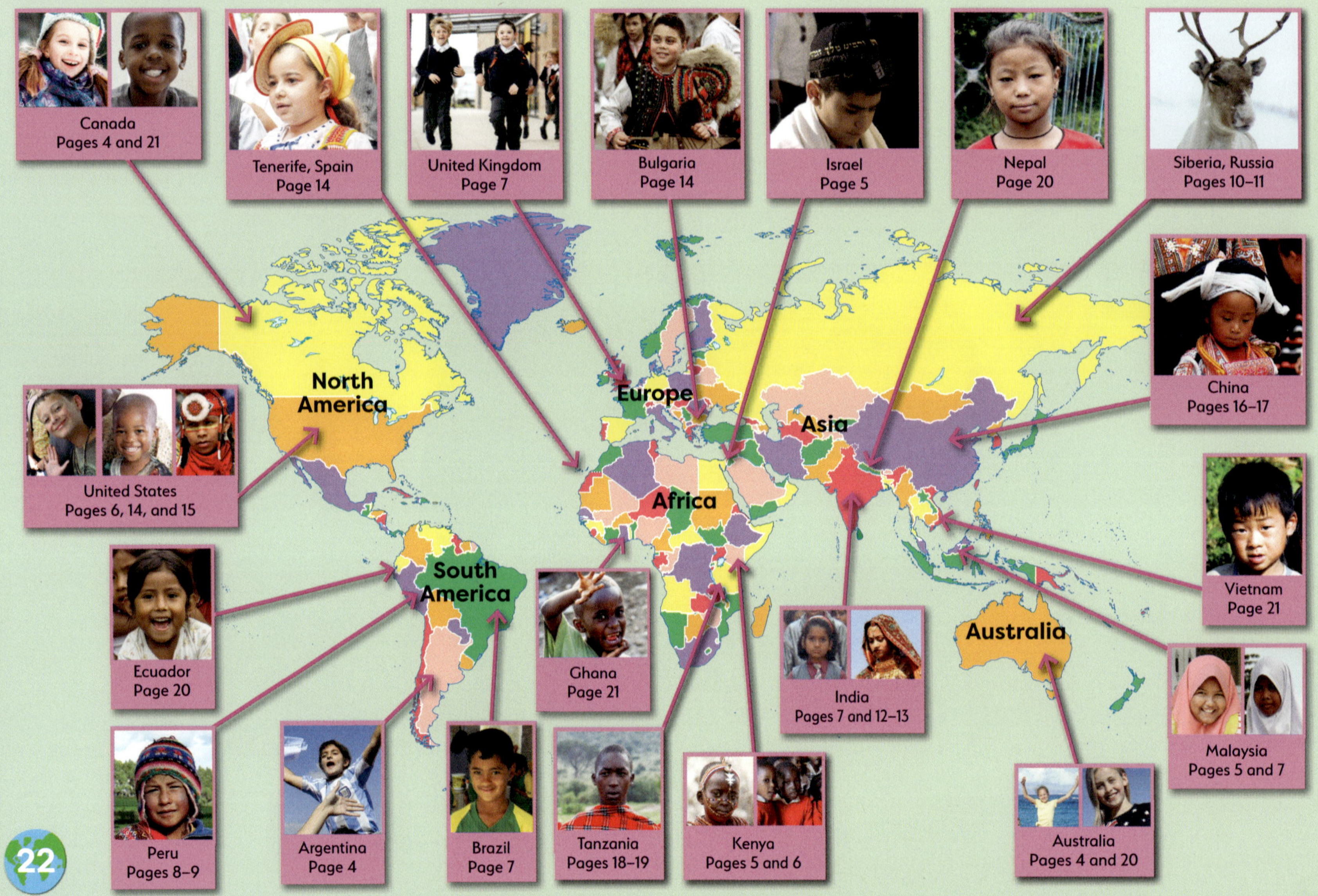

GLOSSARY

ancestor
A relative who lived a long time ago—for example, your great-grandparents and great-great-grandparents are your ancestors.

charity
An organization that raises money and uses it to do good work, such as helping people living in poverty.

embroidery
Creating a picture or pattern on a piece of cloth by making many small stitches with thread.

herder
A person who spends their life caring for animals and moving, or herding, them from place to place so that the animals have enough to eat.

powwow
A ceremony in North America where large numbers of Native people, usually from many tribes, gather to feast, dance, sing, and honor the traditions of their ancestors.

traditional
Something that has been done in a certain way for many years by a group of people—for example, wearing certain clothes or celebrating a particular event.

weave
To make fabric from long pieces of wool by tightly threading, or weaving, them together.

INDEX

A
alpacas 8–9

B
Brazil 7, 22
Bulgaria 14, 22

C
charities 20
China 16–17, 22

E
embroidery 12–13

F
festivals 12, 14, 16

I
India 7, 12–13, 22

K
Kenya 6, 18, 22

L
Long Horn Miao people 16–17

M
Maasai people 18–19

N
Nenets people 10–11

P
Peru 8–9, 22
powwows 15

Q
Quechua people 8–9

R
reindeer 10–11

S
saris 12–13
school uniforms 6–7
shoes and boots 9, 10, 19
Siberia, Russia 10, 22

T
T-shirts 4, 20–21
Tanzania 18–19, 22

U
United Kingdom 7, 22
United States 6, 22